The Churning
Inner Leadership
Workbook

Tools for Building Inspiration
In Times of Change

Finn Jackson

Hertford Street Press

CONTENTS

PREFACE TO THE SECOND EDITION

This second edition of the *Inner Leadership Workbook* has been updated to match the second edition of *The Churning, Volume 1: Inner Leadership*. It also contains a whole new chapter, for people who want to take their inner leadership to the next level.

After practicing the tools of *Inner Leadership* for while we learn to shift our attention away from the individual tools to how we combine and integrate them as a holistic framework. This enables us to create three additional benefits: joy for ourselves, competitive advantage for our organisations, and a more stable generative sustainable economy. The new chapter provides tools that enable us to do this.

Seven Capabilities of Inner Leadership

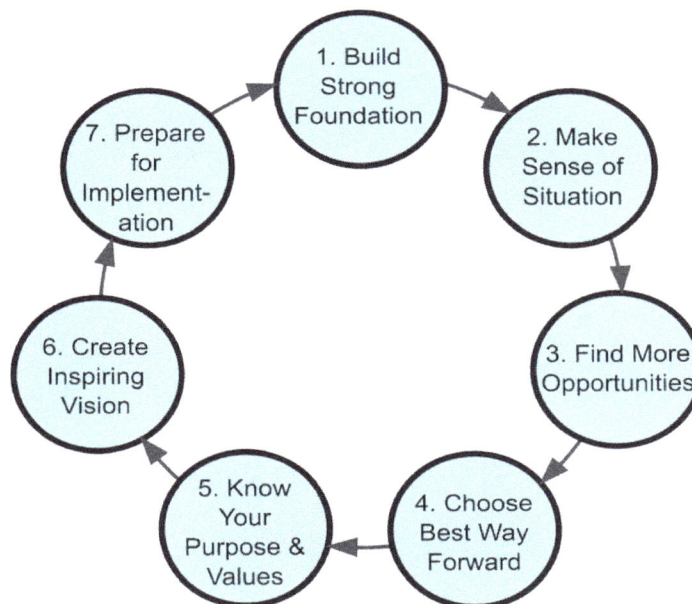

INTRODUCTION

Churning

This workbook accompanies *The Churning, Volume 1: Inner Leadership*. It contains tools, frameworks, and instructions that enable you to build inspiration in yourself and others during times of change.

Applying the tools in this workbook will develop the key skills you need to cope and thrive in times of churning. These include:

- Keeping calm in a crisis and making clear sense of the issues you face
- Identifying more alternatives for moving forward
- Converting the best of those opportunities into a vision that inspires you and other people to want to make it happen

Before we begin, how capable or proficient are you currently at each of the seven sets of skills or competencies of inner leadership? Use the worksheet on the next page to record your answers on a scale of 0-10.

Do you see any skills as particular strengths or weaknesses for you?

In which areas do you most want or need to improve?

In which chapters do you expect to gain the most or least benefit?

Applied in order, these skills combine to form a repeating process. Greater ability at one competency improves our skills at the next: a more solid foundation helps us make clearer sense of the situation; being sure of our purpose and values strengthens our vision, which helps to manage our transitions, and then reinforces our foundation again. Our capacity for inner leadership grows and accelerates each time we move through a complete cycle.

So ask yourself whether your strengths cluster together at the beginning, middle, or end of the process.

Are they roughly equal across all stages?

Is there a gap in your abilities that makes it difficult to move through a complete cycle?

Depending on your current capabilities and the situation you now face, some chapters will be more useful than others. Apply the tools that seem most beneficial today and spend less time on the rest. But remember that what seems less useful today may become more useful tomorrow and each step also builds towards what comes later. So do try out each tool at least once, even those that seem less useful now. Then when the day comes that you need a tool you will know it is there and how to use it.

Chapter / Capability:	Current Ability (0-10)	Current Strength, Weakness, or Neutral?	Greatest Need (X)	Expected Benefit (Hi/Med/Lo)
1. Centre, Ground, and Deepen your connection with yourself				
2. Make Sense of the Situation				
3. Find the Opportunities that every challenge contains				
4. Choose the Best Opportunity for you				
5. Check it against your Purpose and Values				
6. Create an Inspiring Vision				
7. Prepare for Implementation				

Rating your current abilities (in Column 1) will enable you at the end of the book to review the progress you have made. Re-entering those same figures in the chart below may help you to highlight how each step builds towards the next, where you think you are already strong, and where you think you have the biggest need and opportunity to grow:

Inner Leadership Skill or State:

1. CENTRE, GROUND, AND DEEPEN

The first step of inner leadership is at once both deceptively simple and incredibly important. It is the ability in any situation to bring ourselves back to a state of calm inner balance, then focus and connect strongly with who we are and what matters most to us.

To achieve, this we learn to centre and ground ourselves, then deepen our self-connection.

Before we begin, on a scale of 0 to 10, how strongly do you rate your current ability to centre and ground yourself in any situation, and to deeply connect with what matters most to you?

How strongly do you rate your current ability to centre and ground yourself in any situation, and connect deeply with what matters most to you? (0-10)	

Step One: Centre

This section contains three tools that enable you to practice centring:
1. Present-moment awareness
2. Tapping
3. The Sedona Method

Begin by recalling a time when it would have been useful for you to have applied these tools: a time when you felt anxious or nervous about a situation but then it turned out well anyway.

Using these tools might not have changed the outcome of the situation but they could have changed the way you *experienced* it. They would have saved you from unnecessary churning.

Being able to centre yourself quickly at will like this creates a platform for making clearer sense of the situation, making better decisions faster, and so becoming more likely to get the outcomes you want.

Briefly recall 1-3 times in the past when you felt nervous about a situation, but then either your nervousness turned out to be unnecessary or unfounded, or you pushed through and succeeded anyway.	

Tool One: Bring Yourself to Present-Moment Awareness

Following the instructions in *Inner Leadership* (page 3), focus on a feeling of inner churning: either one that you are experiencing currently or which happened recently. Then use this worksheet to record your experiences.

Allow yourself to experience your inner churning. Describe it in your own words.	
What are you feeling, in which parts of your body? What thoughts are you thinking? What name would you give to these feelings or emotions?	
What happens if you focus instead on your breathing and slow it down? Take a deep breath.	
Are you reacting to something that is happening around you now? Or are you remembering the past or imagining the future?	
What happens if you then bring your attention back to what is actually happening around you, right now, and describe it to yourself?	

Tool Two: The Sedona Method

To begin this technique, stop for a moment. You can be sitting or standing, with your eyes open or closed.
The process is simple:
- Think about an issue that has been causing you to churn and about which you would like to feel differently
- Focus on where in your body the churning appears and how it feels; notice any thoughts that go with these feelings
- Welcome these thoughts and feelings, allow them to be

Now ask yourself these questions and note your answers:
1. Just for a short time, is it possible that I could feel differently from the way I am feeling? Just for now, could I let these thoughts and feelings go?
2. Do I want to let them go? Would I let them go?
3. When?

Many people find that the level of churning they experience drops dramatically.
Repeat the process as required. Notice your new thoughts and feelings and where they are in your body. Then ask yourself, "Just for now, could I let these thoughts and feelings go? Would I? When?"

Think about an issue that has been causing you to churn and that you would like to feel freer about. Notice how it feels and where it is in your body. Are there any thoughts associated with the feelings?	
Just for now, could you let these thoughts and feelings go? Would you let them go? When?	
What thoughts and feelings do you have now?	

Tool Three: Tapping or Emotional Freedom Technique

Tapping or Emotional Freedom Technique (EFT) releases negative emotions by tapping our fingers on various acupressure points around the body. Like mindfulness, this can seem a little strange at first. But it works. Millions of people around the world have already benefitted from Tapping. For us it provides a reliable fallback position: a way to ensure we can become centred in even the most extreme circumstances.

To begin:
- Find a place where you can be undisturbed for a few minutes
- Focus on a feeling of churning you would like to release, perhaps something you've experienced over the past few days
- Notice where in your body you are feeling the churning and what it feels like. If you had to name it as an emotion, what would you call it?

Now follow these steps:
- Hold up one hand with the palm facing towards you. Gently start to tap the fleshy side of that hand (the karate chop point) with the fingertips of your other hand.
- As you tap, say out loud three times, "Even though I have this feeling, I deeply and completely love and accept myself." This is called the setup.
- Using your fingertips again, tap the top of your head seven times and as you do so say once, "This feeling."
- Then, using only your first two fingers, tap between your eyebrows seven times and say, "This feeling."
- Repeat this by tapping seven times at the side of your eye, under the eye, and on the upper lip beneath your nose, each time saying, "This feeling."
- Then do the same on your chin, the side of your collarbone, the side of your ribs, and then the inside of your other wrist.
- Now hold up your first hand again but this time with the palm turned away from you. Using only your first finger tap the bottom of the thumbnail seven times and say, "This feeling."
- Then tap the bottom of the nail of the first finger, middle finger, and then skip to your little finger, each time saying, "This feeling" and tapping seven times.
- Now pause and focus on the sensations you were feeling. Have they reduced or gone away? Can you bring the feelings back?

If you want to repeat the process, start again from tapping the top of your head onwards, saying each time, "This feeling."

Use this space to make any notes about your experiences of tapping:	

Present-moment awareness, the Sedona Method, and Tapping (or EFT) provide three reliable techniques for us to be able to centre ourselves when we need to.

All we have to do is remember to use them.

Which of the techniques of Present-Moment Awareness, the Sedona Method, and Tapping will you use to centre yourself?	
How will you remind yourself to remember to apply them when you need them?	

Step Two: Ground

Having centred yourself and restored your balance, the next step is to ground that state. Connect strongly with your best self. The way to do that is by developing a solid anchor.

Tool Four: Anchoring

This tool has five parts or stages.

1) Remember a Time When You Felt Especially Grounded

Remember a time when you felt especially alive, in full flow, sure of who you are, and operating to the maximum of your ability and potential. It doesn't necessarily have to be a time when you were working. Choose an occasion it would be useful to remind yourself of when you find yourself facing a stressful situation or challenge: a time when you felt extremely, solidly grounded in yourself.

Answer these questions:

- Where were you? Who were you with?
- What were you doing? What were you working to achieve? Why?
- How was your body positioned? What was your posture? How were you holding your arms, back, and head? How were you breathing?
- What did it feel like to be so grounded? Could you see, hear, taste, smell, or feel anything special?

Recreate the way your body was positioned then. Does that change how grounded you feel now?

Repeat this for one to three occasions. Focus on what was most important about each one and jot down brief notes for each occasion. Then look for similarities between the experiences and answer the final question, overleaf, to identify what lies at the core essence of being grounded for you.

Occasion 1: (Context, goals, body position)	
Occasion 2: (Context, goals, body position)	
Occasion 3: (Context, goals, body position)	

Describe the Core Essence of being grounded for you:	

2) Solid Pose

To get into solid pose:
- Stand with your feet shoulder width apart, knees slightly bent, and your back straight.
- Feel your weight passing down through your feet into the ground or floor.
- Imagine an invisible thread coming out of the top of your head, pulling your head and neck upwards.

This is a very stable stance, solid, with a low centre of gravity.

Sway slightly from side to side or ask a friend to nudge you. Notice how you feel. Does this position feel more or less grounded than before?

Shift between Solid Pose and your own Grounded Pose and notice the differences.

How does Solid Pose feel to you?	
Do you feel more or less grounded than before? In what ways?	

3) Copy a Person You Admire

Now let's compare your experience of these positions with the behaviour of the most grounded person you can think of. Who is that?

Remember that leadership is an attitude of mind, not a position in an organisation.

Imagine that person in your role. What would her posture be? How would he hold himself? How would she move? How would he speak?

Copy the stance and posture of this person. Stand and behave as they would. Notice how you feel.

Make notes on the next page.

Most Grounded Person: Who is this person? How would they behave? How does copying that feel to you?	
Another Person: Repeat for a second person if you wish.	

4) Choose What's Best for You

Compare how you felt imagining the people you admire with how you felt in Solid Pose and how you felt recreating times from your life when you felt most grounded:
- In which position do you feel most grounded?
- Are there any thoughts, feelings, images, smells, sounds, or tastes that are important for you?
- Now shift into a position that combines the best of everything you have experienced, one that most strongly encapsulates the feeling of being grounded for you.
- Combine it with any images, smells, sounds, or tastes that are important for you.
- Hold that stance for a few moments. Notice how you feel.

The key elements it takes for you to feel most grounded:	
How you feel when you combine those elements:	

5) Create an Anchor to Recall This State at Will

It won't be appropriate to take on your preferred position in every situation where you want to, so we need to find a way to associate it, or 'anchor' it, with something else.

One way is to recall a key word, name, thought, or image and associate that with the feeling of being grounded. If this works for you, choose such a word or image now and write it in the worksheet below.

Another way is to create a physical anchor that can be activated by touching part of your body.

To create a physical anchor:
- Choose a part of your body (for example, your chin, a fingertip, a knuckle).
- Touch that part of your body with a finger, thumb, or perhaps hold it between thumb and forefinger. Touching in this way is what forms the anchor.
- Choose something that will look natural and inconspicuous so you can use it anywhere (for example bringing the fingertips of both hands together or touching your chin with a finger).

To create the anchor:
- Get yourself into the position or think of the word, name, image, smell, sound, or taste that is important for you
- Make the feeling of being grounded as strong as you can
- As you hold your grounded position, image, or thought, set up the anchor you have chosen

- Hold the position, image, or thought while you focus on the feelings of groundedness
- Move out of the position and relax, focus on something else, maybe count to ten
- Return to your highly grounded state and reinitiate the anchor

Repeat this cycle until the anchor becomes associated with the feelings of being grounded. This might take a while. You can develop the anchor to become stronger over time.

How strong an association have you formed with the desired state you want to be able to return to quickly? What level do you want to achieve in the short and long term? What steps will you take to achieve that, when?

The anchor you have chosen: (word, image, or position)	
How you feel when you apply it:	
How strong is your current anchor? (0-10)	
What level is it a priority for you to reach in the short and long term? (0-10)	
What steps will you take to achieve that? When?	

You now have techniques that enable you to centre and ground quickly and at will, letting go of any churning and returning to a state where you feel especially alive and connected, in full flow, sure of who you are, and operating to the maximum of your potential and ability.

The next step is to develop an even deeper connection with yourself.

Step Three: Deepen

Learning to recover quickly from churning is important, but it is better not to experience churning in the first place. Like a tree putting down deeper roots, deepening our groundedness and connectedness to ourselves will make us less likely to be blown over. It will also enable us to spread our leadership branches wider, growing into larger challenges and roles. The more you apply and practise the lessons of this section, the more you will get out of the later chapters.

Tools Five, Six, and Seven:
Physical Exercise, Meditation, and Creativity

Review the material in the section of *Inner Leadership* on deepening your connection with yourself, pages 8 to 12. Make notes about the actions you decide to take. Remember, you can always try something out, find out what happens, and then change again later.

How important is it to you currently to deepen your connection with yourself? Why?	
How much time will you allocate to achieving that?	
What form(s) of physical exercise will you do more of? When?	
What form(s) of meditation will you do more of? When?	
What form(s) of creative activity will you do more of? When?	

Tool Eight: Notice Your Reflection in the World

Use this space to note reminders of:
- *Quotations*, *sayings*, key *facts*, *art*, or *music* that help you to centre and ground or inspire you to action – that remind you what is true and what you care most about
- *Principles* that hold true for you, *values* that are important to you
- Key *facts* (in your work or in the world at large) that consistently make you feel *angry* or *inspired*, or that *provoke you* into taking action

Expand the list as these items come up in your daily life. Combine and reword them. Weed out those that no longer matter. Keep those that have the most meaning for you.

Over time you will build an evolving list of what you care most about, what you believe in, and what you want to create instead. This will also be useful in the later chapters.

Measurement

Having read Chapter 1 and completed the exercises, how strongly do you now rate your ability to centre and ground yourself in any situation, and connect deeply with what matters most to you? (0-10)	

What difference will this make in your life? Professionally? Personally?	
What benefits will that bring? Emotionally? Financially?	
How valuable is that to you?	

2. MAKE SENSE OF THE SITUATION

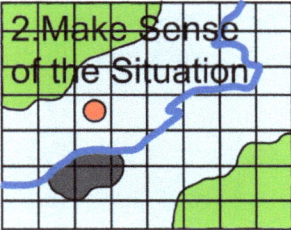

Having centred and deeply grounded, the next step is to make sense of the situation you face. This chapter provides two tools to improve your ability to do that.

Before we begin:

What is your current ability to leverage the power of your unconscious intuition and to identify and make sense of your unconscious and emotional reactions? (0-10)	

Accessing the Power of Our Unconscious Intuition

When the world is changing rapidly, your unconscious mind will often spot patterns before your rational mind does.

One way to access this unconscious intuition is simply to notice how your body feels as you review the alternatives you are considering. Which does it seem to answer 'yes' or 'no' to?

Another way is to toss a coin and see what answer you get. Then notice whether you feel pleased or disappointed with the result.

With practice, intuition can provide a short cut to finding the answers that inspire you most. Then you can still use your rational mind to think those answers through and decide which route to take.

Tool One: Morning Pages

A more structured approach is to use the Morning Pages tool. This involves sitting down with pen and paper first thing in the morning (before your conscious mind is fully awake) and writing out whatever comes into your mind until you have filled three sides of paper. Then make a note of any insights you have uncovered and get on with your day. Pages 19-21 of *Inner Leadership* contain a fuller description.

The Deepening exercises of Chapter 1 will develop your ability to connect with your intuition.

Use this space to make notes about your experience of the three approaches described above.

How clear are the messages your body sends you when you consider different alternatives or when you toss a coin? How reliable do these signals later turn out to be?	
If you wait a few days or weeks, do the messages remain consistent? Have the deepening activities you chose in Chapter 1 developed your ability to make sense of these signals?	
Use this space to make notes about your experience of using the Morning Pages tool. Does your experience of it change over time?	

Unpacking Our Unconscious Reactions

The tool in this section will enable you to identify your mis-blinks, unscramble them, and make clearer sense of the situation. The deeper understanding that you gain as a result will also deepen the centring and grounding you began in Chapter 1 and enhance your use of the Morning Pages tool.

Tool Two: Resolving Our Mis-blinks

To find out whether any of the eight types of mis-blink is distorting your thinking follow these nine steps:

1. Write a short factual description of the situation or what has happened. For example, "Our factory has flooded" or "Person X shouted at me on the phone."
2. Underneath that description, draw five columns. (See the worksheet on the next page.)
3. In the first column, write your interpretations of the event. What are the implications of this event? What does it mean? What, especially, does it mean about you? What, in a few words, are the thoughts that are making you churn? List them all.
4. In the second column, on a scale of 0 to 10, write how sure you are that each thought or interpretation is correct. How likely is each one to be true?
5. Now compare the first of your interpretations (Column 1) with the eight common mis-blinks. Might your interpretation include any mis-blinks? If it might, write their names or numbers in the third column. If you are unsure, write down those you think might apply. The more you include, the greater your chances of finding alternative viewpoints and explanations.
6. For each of these potential mis-blinks, use the descriptions and examples on pages 22 to 35 of *Inner Leadership* to identify alternative explanations that might also be true. Write these in the fourth column. These are your possible "more realistic thoughts."
7. In the fifth column, again on a scale of 0 to 10, write how confident you are that each new interpretation or realistic might be correct. How likely is each one to be true?
8. Repeat steps 5, 6, and 7 for all the thoughts and interpretations you noted in the first column.
9. Look again at the thoughts and interpretations you wrote in the first column. Compare them with the new interpretations you now have in column 4. How likely do you now think your original interpretations are? Add this to Column 2 (step 4).

You hopefully now have a new, deeper understanding of your situation. You have probably found other ways of interpreting what has happened and seen that your original thoughts might not be as certain as you thought. Hopefully you now feel more positive, less constrained, and can see that there is wider scope and more possibilities for taking action to create the results you want.

Tool Two: Resolving Mis-blinks (Sheet 1)

1. Short factual description of the situation you want more clarity on, what happened:				
3. Your interpretation(s) of what happened, what it means or implies:	4. How Likely? (0-10)	5. Possible Mis-Blinks (#1 to 8)	6. What other explanations and interpretations are also possible?	7. How Likely? (0-10)

Tool Two: Resolving Mis-blinks (Sheet 2)

1. Short factual description of the situation you want more clarity on, what happened:			
3. Your interpretation(s) of what happened, what it means or implies:	4. How Likely? (0-10)	5. Possible Mis-Blinks (#1 to 8)	6. What other explanations and interpretations are also possible?	7. How Likely? (0-10)

Measurement

If you have experienced any churning while working on this chapter, remember to use the tools of Chapter 1 to centre and ground and reconnect deeply with what is most important to you.

Having read Chapter 2 and completed the exercises, how strongly do you now rate your ability to leverage the power of your unconscious intuition and to identify and make sense of your unconscious and emotional reactions? (0-10)	

What differences will this make in your life? Professionally? Personally?	
What benefits will that bring? Emotionally? Financially?	
How valuable is that to you?	

3. FIND MORE OPPORTUNITIES

```
3.Identify
Opportunities
●  _____
●  _____
●  _____
●  _____
●  _____
●  _____
●  _____
●  _____
```

Having centred, grounded, and made sense of the situation, the next step is to decide how to move forward. To do that, we first need to identify alternatives. This chapter expands our ability to find those alternatives.

Before we begin:

How strongly do you rate your current ability to find the opportunities in a crisis? (0-10)	

The Problem Is the Opportunity

Many of our greatest inventions and discoveries and have been borne out of difficult situations. We all face frustrations and adversity from time to time but our greatest innovators share something in their inner attitudes that enables them to see opportunity where others see only problems.

Three simple tools can boost our abilities to do the same and make us more likely to spot the opportunities around us. They won't all be applicable in every situation, and they may take time to develop, but applying them will develop your abilities to find the best way forward out of any situation.

Tool One: Daily Appreciation for Serendipity

We become more likely to experience serendipity if we change the way we view the world.

To achieve this shift, set aside five minutes towards the end of each day to identify three to five things that have gone well and for which you are grateful. Setting a reminder on your phone can help. Writing down the items will embed the process initially.

Actively praising or complimenting someone each day gets us into the habit of spotting what is going well as well as the problems. It also builds morale.

The activities for developing creativity in Chapter 1 will further develop your ability to spot solutions.

These practices also help us remain more grounded (Chapter 1) and retain perspective (Chapter 2).

How will you remind yourself at the end of each day to review what went well?	
How will you remind yourself to praise and thank the people around you?	
Do you want to assign more time to activities for developing your creativity?	

Tool Two: Morning Pages to Develop Intuition

The Morning Pages tool of Chapter 2 has already given us a structured approach for developing intuition. It can be reapplied here to help find hidden solutions.

Would it be useful for you to apply it now?

Tool Three: Seeing a Problem as an Opportunity

A third way to become better at finding solutions in adversity is to consciously reinterpret each problem as an opportunity.

To achieve this, follow this deceptively simple two step process:

1. First, redefine the problem in a way that generalises it or expands your viewpoint.
(Applying the "Resolving Our Mis-blinks" tool of Chapter 2 can help to achieve this.)
2. Then ask, "Who would find this (so-called) 'problem' useful?" or "How or where would this 'problem' become an 'advantage'?"

Remember the examples in the book (page 45):

• The engineers with the leaking tunnel might have switched from asking, "Who would value 'flooding'?" to asking, "Who would value 'water that has been filtered through a mountain'?"

• Levi Strauss might have switched from asking, "How can we sell these 'tents'?" to asking, "What other uses do people around here have for 'hard-wearing cloth'?"

Describe a problem you face.	
Describe the situation more neutrally, generally, or generically. Expand your viewpoint. (Tool 2 from Chapter 2 might help with this.)	
Who would find this useful? How or where would the 'problem' become an advantage?	

Five Kinds of Opportunities

Tool Four: Identify Your Current Opportunities

To identify your current opportunities, read *Inner Leadership* pages 42 to 56. Then create more generic or generalised viewpoints of the situation you face and what you want instead:
1. Write a short factual description of the situation or what has happened.
2. Create at least one more generalised, more neutral, more objective version of that description. (You might use the second tool of Chapter 2 to find and resolve any mis-blinks or expand your viewpoint of possible interpretations.)
3. Describe the different features of the outcome you want to create. (There is usually more than one aspect of the situation that is making it difficult, so there is more than one measure you would like to improve. Identifying these metrics makes it clearer what you want instead, which helps identify more ways to achieve that.)
4. Write at least one more generalised, more objective description of the outcome(s) you want (the more variations the better).

Then identify at least one specific way in which you could achieve each of the five opportunities:
1. Ignore or Live With the situation
2. Leave or Exit the situation
3. Fix, Maintain, or Restore the situation
4. Improve the situation
5. Transform or Resolve the situation

Start by thinking big. In the worksheet on the next page, the order has been reversed. What would it have taken to stop this situation arising in the first place? What would it take to prevent it arising again? What would it take to use this situation as an opportunity to create something even better than before? What would it take to restore the situation to the way it used to be? How might you exit or live with the situation?

If you find yourself stuck for ideas, try applying Tools One, Two, and Three above.

Alternatively, think of other people or leaders you admire. If they were in your situation, what would they do? How might they have prevented the situation from arising? How would they shift it from being a crisis to an opportunity to create something better? How might they skirt around the situation by ignoring or living with it? And so on.

Use the worksheet to identify as many possibilities as you can.

At this stage it doesn't matter whether or not the ideas you come up with seem to be practical or applicable. The point is to encourage your mind to think outside its current 'box'. Each idea will bring you new understandings of what works for you, what doesn't, and why. That will trigger new ideas.

Once you have created the fullest possible list of alternatives, and the deepest understanding of their relative merits and disadvantages, then you can choose the option that you are most willing to put in the effort to make happen.

For more examples, refer to pages 53 to 55 of *Inner Leadership*.

Tool Four: Identify Your Current Opportunities

Describe a problem **situation** you face.	
Describe that situation more generally or generically.	
Define the characteristics of the **outcome** you want to create.	
Define those outcome(s) in more general terms.	
What would it take to **Resolve** or **Transform** the situation, so that it could not have arisen in the first place or won't arise again?	
How could you **Improve** the situation, compared with how it was before?	
How could you **Fix**, **Restore**, or **Maintain** the situation?	
How might you **Leave** or **Exit** the situation?	
How might you usefully **Ignore** or **Live With** the situation?	

Ask yourself what a person or leader you particularly admire might do.

Five More Opportunities

Tool Five: Identify Alternative Ways to Apply, Improve, or Transform the Way You Lead Yourself and Others

As well as thinking about how we might change the outer situation, it is also useful to think about how we might change our *inner responses to* the situation. What are the different attitudes we might bring to bear and skills with which we might put these attitudes into practice? In other words, as well as thinking about the different *outcomes* we might create it is also useful to think about the different *inputs* we might bring to the situation: the alternative ways in which we might choose to lead ourselves and others.

You already have a set of leadership skills (and skills in other areas) that you use to move your life forward. This section is about identifying ways in which you might choose to apply or develop those skills.

As before, there are five general approaches. To think this through, first copy your description of the situation and the outcome(s) you want to create into the worksheet on the next page. Then think about and identify at least one specific way in which you could choose to:

6. Not-Apply your current leadership skills
7. Remove your leadership skills to somewhere else
8. Apply the leadership and other skills you already have
9. Improve or Develop new abilities to lead yourself, and others
10. Transform your ability to lead, so that you can prevent similar situations from happening again

Use the worksheet on the next page to identify as many possibilities as you can. Again, the order of the questions has been reversed. Start by thinking big. Refer to the examples on pages 57 to 58 of *Inner Leadership*.

As before, it can be useful to think of other leaders and people you admire. If they were in your situation, what would they do? How might they have prevented the situation from arising in the first place? How would they turn the situation into an opportunity to create something better? How might they skirt around the situation by ignoring or living with it or reducing its priority?

It can also be useful to list the specific relevant skills you already have. This may help you to identify different ways in which you could apply, not apply, or add to them.

As before, the point here is not to immediately find "the right answer" but rather to use the framework to identify possibilities and expand your viewpoint. Even the ideas that seem crazy can lead to other ideas and bring deeper understanding. Once you have created a full list of options you can then choose which one(s) you most want to put in the effort to making happen. This is what we shall do in Chapter 4.

Your existing leadership (and other relevant) skills:

Tool Five: Identify Opportunities in the Way You Lead

Describe the problem **situation** you face.	
Describe that situation more generally or generically.	
Define the characteristics of the **outcome** you want to create.	
Define those outcome(s) in more general terms.	
How could you **Transform** your ability to lead, in a way that would stop the issue from arising again?	
How could you **Improve** or **Develop** your abilities to lead yourself or others?	
How could you **Apply** the leadership abilities you already have?	
How might you **Remove** your leadership, take it elsewhere?	
How might you **Not Apply** your leadership skills?	

Ask yourself what a person or leader you particularly admire might do.

Measurement

If you have experienced any churning while working on this chapter, remember to use the tools of Chapter 1 to centre and ground and reconnect deeply with what is most important to you.

Having read Chapter 3 and completed the exercises, how strongly do you now rate your ability to find the opportunities in a crisis? (0-10)	

What differences will this make in your life? Professionally? Personally?	
What benefits will that bring? Emotionally? Financially?	
How valuable is that to you?	

4. CHOOSE WHAT'S BEST FOR YOU

This chapter is about deciding which of the opportunities in Chapter 3 you are going to pursue.

If you have already made your choice, this chapter will help you clarify or reinforce that decision. If you have not yet decided, this chapter will help you to choose.

This chapter is about identifying the way forward that is best for you personally and making the commitment to follow that path. Its tools and exercises also provide important preparation for the later chapters.

Before we begin:

How strongly do you rate your current ability to choose and pursue the best way forward for you? (0-10)	

Why this Choice Matters

Testing What Makes an Opportunity or a Crisis

Remember a crisis or an opportunity you faced. Use the worksheet below to answer these questions:
- What was the situation?
- Did you see it as a crisis or an opportunity?
- Why?
- Was the root cause that you thought you or your team would be seen as more (or less) important/ significant, competent/talented/skilful, or likeable/popular? (See also the lists of word alternatives on page 68 of *Inner Leadership*.)

Do this for at least one opportunity and at least one crisis.

Situation you faced:	Did you interpret it as a **Crisis** or an **Opportunity**?	**Why?**	**Root Cause?** (Significance, Competence, Likeability?)

The parable of the Taoist farmer (page 44) shows that the situation is just the situation. What turns it into an opportunity or a threat is first the interpretation that we make and second the action that we take: the way we choose to respond. That depends on the level of inspiration we create.

Three Tools for Getting Unstuck

This section contains four tools that will help you choose which opportunity from Chapter 3 you are going to pursue.

Before choosing, it is important to be sure that you can overcome the three blockages that might arise:

- Overthinking
- Not being sure who or what you want to become
- Fear

Have you been experiencing any of these blockages? If you have, use the tools from the first three chapters to address them. First centre and ground yourself. Then:

- Clear overthinking by finding and unravelling any mis-blinks (for example, making *assumptions* about what will happen, wondering what you *should* or *shouldn't* do, and the *extreme thinking* of expecting only 'total success' or 'utter failure' instead of something in between)
- Get clearer on what future you prefer and who you most want to become by using the Morning Pages from Chapter 2 or the longer term Deepening exercises of Chapter 1
- Shift your response to fear from "Forget Everything And Run" to "Face Everything And Rise" by using Chapter 3 to find and list your opportunities, then find what inspires you

Have you been experiencing any overthinking, fear, or not knowing what outcome you ultimately want to create? Describe what you have experienced.	Have you applied the relevant tools from the earlier chapters? Did they help to reduce or resolve these issues?

Tool One: Learning from Others

This tool has two parts. For the first part, choose one to three people you have never met but who you greatly admire. They might be people from history or from the present day: role models who taught you something important but who you never interacted with.

For each one, write down or (better) discuss with a close friend or partner:
1. What are the values you admire in these people?
2. What flaws or weaknesses did they have?
3. What, despite those flaws, did they manage to achieve that you admire them for?

Discussing this with someone you trust will enable them to draw out what is important to you by asking open questions such as, "Why? What do you mean by that? Can you give me an example?"

Name of Person:	Their Values:	Their Flaws or Weaknesses:	What They Achieved:

For the second part, choose one to three mentors, managers, leaders, teachers, or friends you have known in real life who taught you something that has helped to shape the person you have become.

For each one, write down or discuss with a close friend or partner:
1. What did these people love that you loved them for loving?
2. What were their flaws or weaknesses?
3. What, despite those flaws, did they managed to achieve that you admire them for?

Name of Person:	What You Loved Them For Loving:	Their Flaws or Weaknesses:	What They Achieved:

Reminding yourself of the qualities and achievements you admire in others will remind you what is important to you and help you choose your way forward.

Your answers also show that even the people we most admire did not have to be perfect in order to achieve something worthwhile. And if they didn't have to be perfect neither do we.

Your answers to both parts of this tool will be important for Chapter 5.

Tool Two: Learning from Your Past

Another way to gain confidence for moving forward is to reexamine and learn from events in the past that *didn't* turn out the way you expected. (In a time of change, this is going to happen a lot.)

Pick one or two times in your life when things didn't turn out the way you thought they would. Remember Thomas Edison who saw each so-called 'failure' as a successful step towards creating what he wanted. For each situation identify briefly:

- What choice did you make? What did you expect was going to happen?
- What actually happened? What lesson did you learn at the time?
- Using Chapter 2, was that lesson a mis-blink? What alternative explanations are also possible? Which seems more likely now?
- What other opportunities might you have chosen – to ignore, leave, fix, improve, or transform the situation or your leadership?
- Would you take the same decision again?

Situation:		
Choice you made, what you expected to happen		
What actually happened that you didn't expect Lesson Learned		
Was this a Mis-blink? Alternative Explanations		
Other Opportunities? (Transform, Improve, Fix, Leave, Ignore)		
Would you take the same decision again?		

If you would take the same decision again then you can trust the decision you make now. If you would take a different decision then you have learned from the experience. Either way, you can trust the decision you make now, knowing that it will either turn out as you expect or provide you with useful learning.

Tool Three: Learning from Your Future

Life doesn't always turn out the way we expect, and as we grow older we generally become wiser. Think about and then answer the following questions.

What advice would you give now to your 6-year-old self?	
What advice would you give now to your 16-year-old self?	
What advice would you give now to your 26-year-old self?	
What advice would your 86-year-old self give to you now?	

The second part of this tool is about defining what a worthwhile life looks like for you. On your deathbed, what will it take for you to have lived a worthwhile life? To have made good use of your time? To have finished well?

To define this, and apply it, read pages 77-78 of *Inner Leadership* and then:
- Identify six to eight categories or areas that are important to whatever living 'a worthwhile life' looks like for you.
- Define what a '10' would look like. What it would take to have achieved everything you could possibly hope to under that heading during your lifetime? (Draw pictures if that helps.)
- On a scale of 0 to 10, where are you for each area or category today?
- What would be appropriately sized steps to move forward over the next week, month, or year? Or what would it take to improve by 0.5 or 0.1 from where you are now?

We all have different interests and start from different places, with different resources at our disposal. We don't all want to be Elon Musk or Michelle Obama. But we are all human becomings. To live whatever a worthwhile life means for you, a good starting point is to know the six to eight areas that matter most to you: the direction you want to face in and the manner in which you want to travel. Then take baby steps.

What will it take for you to live a **Worthwhile Life**?	What '10' would look like in an ideal world:	Where are you today? (0-10)	Appropriately sized steps for the coming week, month, year:

What will it take for you to live a **Worthwhile Life**?	What '10' would look like in an ideal world:	Where are you today? (0-10)	Appropriately sized steps for the coming week, month, year:

Tool Four: Comparing Your Alternatives

Use this tool to compare the upsides and downsides of the top alternatives you are considering from Chapter 3. The tool will enable you to choose between these alternatives or to understand more deeply a choice you have already made.

To use the tool, follow these four steps, filling out your answers on the worksheet across the next three pages:

1. List the top few alternative ways forward that you are considering
2. Think through the upsides of each and rate them as high, very high, low, or very low
   (You want the upsides to be high.)
3. Think through the downsides of each option and rate them as high, very high, low, or very low
   (You want the downsides to be low.)
4. Then ask yourself what is important about the implementation: is it cost, speed, certainty of success, longevity, durability, or some other factor? Whatever the answer, then think about how you would implement each option and give it an "implementation rating" of high, medium, or low; easy, medium, or hard; or perhaps green, amber, or red (where high, easy, and green are what you prefer).

When you have thought through and filled out your answers for each option, map those answers on to the appropriate square or quadrant of the chart on the fourth page. Use different coloured circles or a note in brackets to indicate the implementation rating. (See the example on page 79 of *Inner Leadership*. Shade the background squares if that is useful to you.)

The main value of this exercise comes from thinking through the options, gaining greater clarity on what each one involves and what matters most to you.

Mapping your answers provides a visual summary which often brings yet more clarity.

There is no 'right' or 'best' answer here except what you choose. Only you can define what mix of upsides, downsides, and implementation is right for you now, given the situation you face.

Often you will already know the option you want to take and the chart will provide an explanation or reinforcement of the decision you have already made: the thinking through helps you understand why. This gives you more confidence to move to implementation.

Sometimes, though, this tool will show up a potential flaw in the choice you have made – something you had overlooked or not considered – so it is always a useful check.

Tool 4: Comparing Your Alternatives

Option Name and Description:	What are the Upsides? (Very Low, Low, High, Very High?)	What are the Downsides? (Very Low, Low, High, Very High?)	"Implementation Rating" (Hi/Med/Lo or Green, Amber, Red)

Tool 4: Comparing Your Alternatives

Option Name and Description:	What are the Upsides? (Very Low, Low, High, Very High?)	What are the Downsides? (Very Low, Low, High, Very High?)	"Implementation Rating" (Hi/Med/Lo or Green, Amber, Red)

Tool 4: Comparing Your Alternatives

Option Name and Description:	What are the Upsides? (Very Low, Low, High, Very High?)	What are the Downsides? (Very Low, Low, High, Very High?)	"Implementation Rating" (Hi/Med/Lo or Green, Amber, Red)

Title:

U P S I D E S

	Very High	High	Low	Very Low
Very Low				
Low				
High				
Very High				

DOWNSIDES

Choosing the Best Opportunity for You

Which of the opportunities you identified in Chapter 3 have you chosen as the best way forward for you at the current time? (Not necessarily the 'ideal world' option but the one you can fully commit to.)	
Why is that the best option for you now?	
For the record, how have you made this decision? - What methods or tools did you use to make your decision? - What factor(s) most drove your choice? What aspect did you decide was most important? (eg was it Values, Courage, Learning, Worthwhile Life, Upsides, Downsides, Implementation, Other...?)	

Measurement

If you have experienced any churning while working on this chapter, remember to use the tools of Chapter 1 to centre and ground and reconnect deeply with what is most important to you.

Having read Chapter 4 and completed the exercises, how strongly do you now rate your ability to choose and pursue the best way forward for you? (0-10)	

What differences will this make in your life? Professionally? Personally?	
What benefits will that bring? Emotionally? Financially?	
How valuable is that to you?	

5. KNOW YOUR PURPOSE AND VALUES

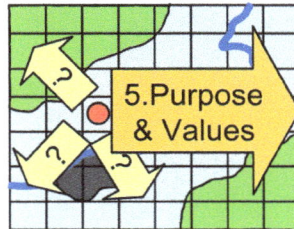

This chapter enables you to define your purpose and values. Knowing them will bring you inner stability, direction, and energy while all around is churning.

Before we begin:

How clear are you currently on what your purpose and values are? (0-10)	

Tool One: Identify Your Purpose in Life

To identify your purpose in life, follow these four steps.

Step 1: Identify Your Two Best Qualities

Start by following this process:
- Ask yourself what are the two main qualities you bring to the world.
- If you find it difficult to pick only two, ask a few trusted friends what qualities they see in you. Listen to their answers, ignore what you don't like, and keep what you do.
- Pick, choose, or combine the rest to come up with the two qualities that you feel best describe you: qualities that you love expressing and which summarise the essence of who you are in the world.

If you're not sure, go with two qualities that feel right for now and try them out. You can always come back and update them later if you want to.

What are the two best qualities you bring to the world?	

Step 2: Say How You Love Expressing these Qualities

Next, identify how you most love applying these qualities. You might express this in different ways so ask yourself these three questions, then use the space below to write what resonates most with you:
- When you are putting your best qualities into practice in the way you most enjoy, what outcomes are you trying to create in the people around you?
- What change are you seeking to make in the world?
- What is the effect you most love to have when you're putting your best qualities into practice?

How do you love expressing your two best qualities?	

Step 3: Define Your Ideal World

Imagine what the world would be like right now if it were perfect, according to you:
- What would you see, hear, feel, taste, or smell?
- What would that mean?
- What kind of a world is that?

What does an ideal world look like to you?	

Step 4: Put It All Together

To find your purpose in life, or a first draft that you can develop over time, take your three answers from above and join them to form a sentence.

For example, you might say:

"The purpose of my life is to use my [**two main qualities**] to [**achieve what you said was the way you love expressing those qualities**], to create [**your ideal world**]."

Or you could change the order to say:

"The purpose of my life is to create [**my ideal world**] by using my [**two main qualities**] to [**make the difference I love to make when expressing those qualities**]."

See pages 90 to 92 of *Inner Leadership* for more details and examples.

Use the space on the next page to make notes and experiment with different formats.

Remember there is no 'right' way of doing this: find the set of words that feels right to you. Then treat that as a "work in progress": try it out, apply it, see what happens, and improve it as you go forward.

My Purpose Statement:

Notes / Working space:

Tool Two: Find Your Values

To connect with your values – the guiding principles that are most important to you – remember a time when you felt fully absorbed in your work. You lost track of time, felt fully alive, in flow, operating at your maximum potential, doing what you are here to do.

- Ask yourself what values were you standing up for in that moment when you felt most alive. What values were you upholding or taking action in support of?
- Write down all the values that come to mind.
- Do this for between one and three occasions.

If you find it difficult to identify the values you were standing for, try thinking of situations where you stood up against something:

- What were you were standing against?
- What values are the opposite of that?

Write down your results.

Occasion:	Values: (Or the opposites of what you stood against)

Working on this exercise with a trusted friend who asks open questions can help you to tease out and clarify your thinking: "Why? What do you mean? Can you give an example?" It will take probably about 10 to 15 minutes for each person to complete the exercise.

You might find it useful to add your answers from the first tool in Chapter 4, where you identified the values you admired in others, what you loved them for loving, the opposites of their flaws, and the things you admired them for achieving. All these are indicators of your values.

Copy your answers from Tool One of Chapter 4 (pages 34-35 of this workbook):

Values you admire in others	
Opposites of their flaws	
What they achieved	
What you loved them for loving	
Opposites of their flaws	
What they achieved	

You now almost certainly have a list of more than three values. Use the space on the next page to group, merge, and combine them until you have distilled them down to find your three core values.

The more effort you put into this activity now the more confident you can be of the results you obtain and the more lasting they will be.

What are the three core values you stand for?

Complete at least a first draft of your purpose and values before continuing.

My Three Core Values:

Notes / Working space:

Applying This New Information

After defining your purpose and values it will probably become clear that you don't always live up to them. This is to be expected: we are, after all, only human and we don't always live in a perfect environment that makes it easy to apply our purpose and values to every aspect of our lives.

But once we know what our purpose and values are, they give us something to aim for. Like the building blocks of our worthwhile life, they provide a direction to face in that we can move towards and see how far we can get, given the times we happen to have been born into.

While you decide what actions to take, you might want to give your purpose and values a chance to settle, to see whether you are happy with what you have created or want to update the wording.

As you do so, ask yourself these questions:

To what extent are you living in line with your purpose and values today?	
What are the main areas of alignment?	
What are the main areas of non-alignment?	

What would your life be like if you lived completely in line with your purpose and values?	
What changes would be easiest to make first? (What would be the upsides and downsides of each?)	
Now think about the opportunity you chose in Chapter 4. Is it in line with your purpose and values? Will pursuing it help you to apply your values and achieve your purpose?	
Is there another opportunity from Chapter 3 that would be more in line with your purpose and values?	
From where you are today, does it make sense to pursue that opportunity instead, or to stick with the one you have already chosen?	
Do you want to update the wording of your purpose or values?	

Measurement

If you have experienced any churning while working on this chapter, remember to use the tools of Chapter 1 to centre and ground and reconnect deeply with what is most important to you.

Having read Chapter 5 and completed the exercises, how clear are you now on what your purpose and values are? (0-10)	

What differences will this make in your life? Professionally? Personally?	
What benefits will that bring? Emotionally? Financially?	
How valuable is that to you?	

6. CREATE AN INSPIRING VISION

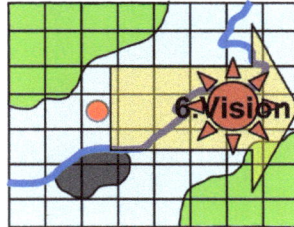

Vision matters. It makes us come alive.

In this chapter there are two activities:

* Learning from leaders you admire
* Creating an inspiring vision for each of your key audiences

Before we begin:

How able are you currently to describe your chosen way forward as an inspiring vision? (0-10)	

Learning from People or Leaders You Admire

Begin by thinking of one or two leaders or other people you admire and a time when they said or did something that inspired you.

What did they say or do that you found inspiring? These are the elements that are most likely to match your style.

Read the box on page 112 of *Inner Leadership* and record your answers in the table on the next page.

Learning from People or Leaders You Admire

Name a leader you admire:		
Think of a time when they said or did something you found inspiring:		
What did you find inspiring about what they said or did, or the way they said or did it?		
Which of the seven building blocks of a vision do these elements correspond to or relate to?		
Is there anything about what the person said and did and how they said or did it that does **not** seem to fit with any of the seven building blocks?		
How can you apply these insights to the situation you currently face and the inspiration you want to create?		

Tool One: Create Your Inspiring Vision

To create an inspiring vision-story for the opportunity you selected in Chapter 4, first make a prioritised list of the audiences or stakeholders whose enthusiastic support you want or need. Put yourself at the top of the list.

List your priority audiences:

1)	Myself
2)	
3)	
4)	
5)	

Use the templates below for each audience you identified. At the top of each worksheet, write the name of the opportunity you are creating a vision-story for and the name of the audience. Then follow these seven steps for each audience, starting with yourself:

1. Read the descriptions of the seven building blocks given in *Inner Leadership* (pages 101-111) and make bullet point notes on how each block might apply to this audience, your current situation, and the opportunity you are inspiring them to pursue.
2. If a building block doesn't seem to apply, leave it and move on. (You might ask yourself why it doesn't apply.)
3. Include any new building blocks you identified in the "Learning from People or Leaders You Admire" worksheet, above. Add bullet point notes on how these might apply to your situation.
4. Review all the bullets and **identify the key points** and themes that stand out as important. Remember, the aim is not to include everything but to create **a story that inspires** this audience.
5. Copy the key points on to the second worksheet for this audience. Regroup and reorder them as you do so, to get a sense of an emerging story.
6. Experiment with putting the points into different orders. Form new phrases, sentences, or paragraphs. Find an order that seems to tell the story you want to tell to this audience. (Copying the key points on to sticky notes or Post-It notes can be a useful way to do this.)
7. Once you have a structure you like, develop your vision-story further. Flesh out the details. Try it out with your chosen audience.
8. Learn and repeat.

Experiment by putting your ideas into different orders. (To encourage this, the first page for each audience uses a different order.) Find your voice and what you think will work best to inspire, engage, and retain each audience. Notice where there is overlap between the visions for different audiences.

Ask yourself what would happen if you tightened or focused all the vision-stories around this shared core. Compare that with what would happen if you kept each vision more distinct and separate.

Create Your Inspiring Vision-Story

Opportunity:	
Audience 1:	Myself

1. Authentically Me	2. Relevant for this Audience	4. Show There Is a Problem	5. Future You Want to Create
6. Principles, Values, Ideals	7. Achievable First Steps	3. Why Make a Decision Now	8. Other Building Block(s)

Combine the Key Elements

Opportunity:	
Audience 1:	Myself

Key Bullet Points:

Capture the main points.

Experiment:

Arrange the key points in different orders to build the vision-story you want to tell this audience.

Create Your Inspiring Vision-Story

Opportunity:	
Audience 2:	

4. Show There Is a Problem	2. Relevant for this Audience	5. Future You Want to Create	
6. Principles, Values, Ideals	3. Why Make a Decision Now	1. Authentically Me	8. Other Building Block(s)
			7. Achievable First Steps

Combine the Key Elements

Opportunity:	
Audience 2:	

Key Bullet Points:
Capture the main points.

Experiment:
Arrange the key points in different orders to build the vision-story you want to tell this audience.

Create Your Inspiring Vision-Story

Opportunity:			
Audience 3:			

2. Relevant for this Audience	4. Show There Is a Problem	3. Why Make a Decision Now	7. Achievable First Steps
6. Principles, Values, Ideals	5. Future You Want to Create	1. Authentically Me	8. Other Building Block(s)

Combine the Key Elements

Opportunity:	
Audience 3:	

Key Bullet Points:
Capture the main points.

Experiment:
Arrange the key points in different orders to build the vision-story you want to tell this audience.

Create Your Inspiring Vision-Story

Opportunity:	
Audience 4:	

6. Principles, Values, Ideals	5. Future You Want to Create	2. Relevant for this Audience	7. Achievable First Steps
4. Show There Is a Problem	3. Why Make a Decision Now	1. Authentically Me	8. Other Building Block(s)

Combine the Key Elements

Opportunity:	
Audience 4:	

Key Bullet Points:
Capture the main points.

Experiment:
Arrange the key points in different orders to build the vision-story you want to tell this audience.

Create Your Inspiring Vision-Story

Opportunity:	
Audience 5:	

	1. Authentically Me	2. Relevant for this Audience	4. Show There Is a Problem
3. Why Make a Decision Now			
5. Future You Want to Create	6. Principles, Values, Ideals	7. Achievable First Steps	8. Other Building Block(s)

Combine the Key Elements

Opportunity:	
Audience 5:	

Key Bullet Points:

Capture the main points.

Experiment:

Arrange the key points in different orders to build the vision-story you want to tell this audience.

Measurement

If you have experienced any churning while working on this chapter, remember to use the tools of Chapter 1 to centre and ground and reconnect deeply with what is most important to you.

Having read Chapter 6 and completed the exercises, how able are you now to describe your chosen way forward as an inspiring vision-story? (0-10)	

What differences will this make in your life? Professionally? Personally?	
What benefits will that bring? Emotionally? Financially?	
How valuable is that to you?	

7. PREPARE FOR THE JOURNEY

As you and your team work to implement your vision, you will all go through three stages of transition. Some of these transitions will be large, others small.

This chapter readies you to manage those transitions and maintain inspiration in yourself and your team, by providing tools that enable you to:

- Move smoothly through the three phases: Separation, Threshold, Consolidation
- Build a map of the key landmarks of *Inner Leadership*, to guide you as you move forward

Before we begin:

How well-prepared are you now to deal with the inner leadership issues that will arise as you implement the outcome you chose in Chapter 4? (0-10)	

Managing the Transitions

Tool One: Managing the Separation Phase

Start by remembering a time when you lost something or someone that was important to you. Answer these questions to remind yourself of what others on your team might be going through and the benefits of helping them to reach closure.

Remember a time when you lost something or someone that was important to you but from which you have now moved on and separated.	
Who or what did you lose? What did that mean to you? How did the loss impact you at the time?	
What difference has successful Separation made, in how you feel and what you can achieve? What would be the impact for your project if your team could achieve the same more quickly?	
How long did it take for you to get over your loss? What made the difference that enabled you to move on?	
What does all this teach you about the situation you face now, in terms of: - Appreciating what others may be feeling - Valuing the benefits of achieving Separation - Assisting people to make this change	

Separation – First Audience

Use these questions to think through how you can assist your most important audience or stakeholder (yourself) to achieve Separation from your past.

Group or individual important to achieving your vision:	Myself
How far has this group Separated from the past (0-10)? How do you know? What would '10' look like?	
What do they most value from the past? What does that mean* to them?	
How can you help this audience give thanks for what has been, accept that it has gone, and show that this meaning is being rebuilt as part of the future vision?	
What events or rituals could symbolise the ending of the old phase and the beginning of the new? When would be a good time for this? Where and how?	

* Consider Maslow's hierarchy of needs: safety, belonging, esteem, respect, self-actualisation, identity.

Separation – Second Audience

Use these questions to think through how you can assist the second key audience or stakeholder group, important to your vision, to achieve Separation from their past.

Group or individual important to achieving your vision:	
How far has this group Separated from the past (0-10)? How do you know? What would '10' look like?	
What do they most value from the past? What does that mean* to them?	
How can you help this audience give thanks for what has been, accept that it has gone, and show that this meaning is being rebuilt as part of the future vision?	
What events or rituals could symbolise the ending of the old phase and the beginning of the new? When would be a good time for this? Where and how?	

* Consider Maslow's hierarchy of needs: safety, belonging, esteem, respect, self-actualisation, identity.

Separation – Third Audience

Use these questions to think through how you can assist the third key audience or stakeholder group, important to your vision, to achieve Separation from their past.

Group or individual important to achieving your vision:	
How far has this group Separated from the past (0-10)? How do you know? What would '10' look like?	
What do they most value from the past? What does that mean* to them?	
How can you help this audience give thanks for what has been, accept that it has gone, and show that this meaning is being rebuilt as part of the future vision?	
What events or rituals could symbolise the ending of the old phase and the beginning of the new? When would be a good time for this? Where and how?	

* Consider Maslow's hierarchy of needs: safety, belonging, esteem, respect, self-actualisation, identity.

Separation – Fourth Audience

Use these questions to think through how you can assist the fourth key audience or stakeholder group, important to your vision, to achieve Separation from their past.

Group or individual important to achieving your vision:	
How far has this group Separated from the past (0-10)? How do you know? What would '10' look like?	
What do they most value from the past? What does that mean* to them?	
How can you help this audience give thanks for what has been, accept that it has gone, and show that this meaning is being rebuilt as part of the future vision?	
What events or rituals could symbolise the ending of the old phase and the beginning of the new? When would be a good time for this? Where and how?	

* Consider Maslow's hierarchy of needs: safety, belonging, esteem, respect, self-actualisation, identity.

Separation – Fifth Audience

Use these questions to think through how you can assist the fifth key audience or stakeholder group, important to your vision, to achieve Separation from their past.

Group or individual important to achieving your vision:	
How far has this group Separated from the past (0-10)? How do you know? What would '10' look like?	
What do they most value from the past? What does that mean* to them?	
How can you help this audience give thanks for what has been, accept that it has gone, and show that this meaning is being rebuilt as part of the future vision?	
What events or rituals could symbolise the ending of the old phase and the beginning of the new? When would be a good time for this? Where and how?	

* Consider Maslow's hierarchy of needs: safety, belonging, esteem, respect, self-actualisation, identity.

Tool Two: Crossing the Threshold

Having let go of the past, you and your team can now start to build the future. Your role here is to provide structure that enables people to cope with uncertainty.

A) Bottom-Up: The Skills of Inner Leadership

One way to achieve this is bottom-up, by giving each person the skills to manage their own uncertainty.
Use the table below to evaluate:
- How important each audience or stakeholder group is to the success of your vision
- How capable they currently are at the skills of *Inner Leadership*, especially Chapters 1 to 3
- What actions, if any, you will take as a result

Key audience, group, or individual important to achieving your vision	Importance (0-10)	Current Ability at Chapters 1-3 (0-10)	Actions, When
Myself			

B) Top-Down: Instilling Culture

Another way to achieve this is top-down, by defining and instilling a culture of clear values that guide daily attitudes and behaviour.

Start by listing the values that might be important to achieving and maintaining your vision. As you do so, group or cluster them to find the three to five underlying themes or core values that are most essential to your vision.

List the values that are important to your vision. **Group or cluster those that are similar or related.**	
The three to five fundamental underlying values most essential to the success of your finished vision:	

On the next page, convert these values into specific attitudes and behaviours that are important for each audience or stakeholder. How will you know when people are putting the values into practice?

Do your proposed actions demonstrate the values? Do they show the values as well as tell them?

Key audiences important to achieving your vision	Values most relevant to this individual or group's contribution	Attitudes and behaviours that would demonstrate these values	Current Performance (0-10)	Action, When
Myself				

Tool Three: Managing Consolidation

This tool has four parts:
- Communicating milestones
- Creating shared understanding
- Building shared purpose
- Getting to closure

Communicating Milestones

In the Consolidation phase you focus on showing that progress is being made and on shaping what that progress means to the various audiences or stakeholders whose support you need on the journey to your vision.

Use the worksheets on the following pages to create a high level communications plan for your project. Use one sheet for each audience (group or individual). Convert these summaries into more detailed plans in whatever way is appropriate to your project.

For each audience, start by listing in the left column the relevant milestones (large and small) on the way to your vision. Start with the current quick wins.

Then, for each milestone, answer the following:
1. Why does this milestone matter to this audience? Why do they care about it? Why is it important to *them*? What would it mean to them if the milestone was achieved or not achieved?
2. Why is it important to you or the project what this audience thinks about this milestone and that they know when it has happened? What actions might they take or not take? What action do you want them to take?
3. What will you communicate to this audience about this milestone and what it means? When and how will you do that?
4. How will you monitor the effectiveness of your communications at achieving Consolidation?

You can expect different milestones to be relevant for different audiences, for different reasons. Customise the worksheets accordingly.

The way that you apply this tool for the first audience, "Myself," is slightly different from the others. For you, this tool brings clarity on which milestones most impact the future direction of the project and how they do so (Column 2). It also shows which milestones impact your ability to be effective in your role and why (Column 3). Any event that won't impact the direction of the project or your ability to perform your role is not really a 'milestone', it's just a tick box. So, for the first audience, "Myself," this tool helps to highlight which milestones matter, why, and what information you need to know in order to make the necessary decisions and fulfil your role.

For the other audiences, this tool helps to identify and manage the key events that will most shape the ongoing engagement of those audiences with your project. It may also show where you need communication to happen between milestone events.

Communicating Milestones, Audience 1

Audience:	Myself			
Milestone	Why this milestone matters to the project, its implications	Why I care, How this milestone impacts my ability to fulfil my role	What I need to know about this milestone, when and how	How we will monitor milestone reporting effectiveness

Communicating Milestones, Audience 2

Audience:				
Milestone	Why this audience cares about this milestone, what it means to them	Why this audience's under-standing matters to the project	What you will communicate, when, how	How you will monitor effectiveness

Communicating Milestones, Audience 3

Audience:				
Milestone	Why this audience cares about this milestone, what it means to them	Why this audience's under-standing matters to the project	What you will communicate, when, how	How you will monitor effectiveness

Communicating Milestones, Audience 4

Audience:				
Milestone	Why this audience cares about this milestone, what it means to them	Why this audience's under-standing matters to the project	What you will communicate, when, how	How you will monitor effectiveness

Communicating Milestones, Audience 5

Audience:				
Milestone	Why this audience cares about this milestone, what it means to them	Why this audience's under-standing matters to the project	What you will communicate, when, how	How you will monitor effectiveness

Creating Shared Understanding of the Overall Plan

Collaboration, cooperation, and consistency are more likely if people understand the overall plan. But not all audiences need to understand the whole picture. Use this worksheet to think through the benefits to the project of each audience or stakeholder having understanding the whole plan. Identify the level of understanding they currently have (0-10), what is missing, and what actions you will take to address this.

Audience, individual, or group	How much of the overall plan you need them to understand, and why	Current performance (0-10) Gap or Needed Improvement	Actions, When
Myself			

Building Shared Purpose

Purpose is a way to align the decision-making of the different groups and individuals involved in making your vision real. Knowing the purpose enables them to act independently, quickly, yet remain in alignment. This is achieved best by defining a single overall shared purpose but you might also want to define a purpose specific to each individual or group.

Start by defining the overall purpose of your vision.

What is the purpose of your finished vision:	

On the next page, define how this applies to each of your key audiences:
- What is the role or contribution that each group or individual makes? How clearly do they understand or appreciate that role and its mutual interdependencies with other parts of the project (0-10)?
- Does the purpose of the project motivate and inspire them each day? Do they use it to shape or control the decisions they take?
- Would it be beneficial for this audience or stakeholder to develop a clearer understanding of the purpose of the project and how it applies to them? Would it be useful to define a separate purpose specific to them or to develop the values, attitudes, and behaviours defined earlier (page 80)?
- What actions will you take to develop a sense of shared purpose for this audience?

Building Shared Purpose

Key individual or group important to achieving your vision	Role they play, and their current appreciation of that role and its interdependencies (0-10)	Does the Purpose motivate them? Does it shape their decisions? (0-10)	How best to develop the sense of shared Purpose in this audience?	Actions, When
Myself				

(See also the values, attitudes, and behaviours defined on page 80.)

Getting to Closure

If the opportunity you chose in Chapter 4 was to achieve a single outcome, the Consolidation stage finishes when that end is in sight. If you chose to build a new entity, Consolidation finishes when it stops being a project and starts being a viable ongoing organisation.

What event will signify for you that the Consolidation stage is complete?	
What milestones remain until that point is reached?	
Which of those milestones, and what associated actions, will have most impact on successfully achieving consolidation?	
What comes next after Consolidation is complete?	

A Map to Guide You

No one has ever tried to create your vision before, not in the way that you have defined it, and not in the circumstances you now face. By pulling together the key landmarks of *Inner Leadership* you prepare yourself emotionally to deal with whatever happens as you work to make your vision a reality.

Use the next two pages to create a handy reference map of the key highlights of *Inner Leadership*. The page numbers show where to find the key information in this workbook and copy it here.

Whenever you encounter difficulties this map will enable you quickly to remember your priorities, renew your focus, and move forward to achieve your vision, values, and purpose.

Remember also the importance of continuing to Centre and Ground yourself as each new issue arises. Each one is an opportunity to Deepen your connection with yourself over time.

Map of Key Landmarks

(To be used for re-orientation, as needed)

Name: ....

Date: ....

Purpose and Values (Pages 50, 53)

My purpose in life is to ....

....

....

The values that are important to me in achieving that are ....

Opportunity (Page 45)

The opportunity I have chosen as the best way to achieve that purpose now is ....

....

My Vision of that Opportunity (Pages 60-61 and following)

Authenticity for me is about ....

....

I am looking for ....

....

Reality of the situation is that ....

....

The future we are going to create ....

....

Relevant higher principle(s), value(s) and ideal(s) ....

....

The achievable first steps are ....

....

I can convince myself to make a decision now by ....

....

Map of Key Landmarks

(To be used for re-orientation, as needed)

Managing the Transitions (Page 59 and Chapter 7)

Key individuals and groups
important to my vision

....

....

Transition stage they are
currently in

....

....

Priorities for successful transition ....

....

Oxygen Masks

When I encounter churning, I
centre myself by

....

(Page 6)

The anchor I use to ground
myself is

....

(Page 11)

I deepen my connection with
myself by

....

(Page 12)

Things that inspire me ....

(Page 13)

Motivators and facts that spur me
to action

....

(Page 13)

What It Will Take for Me to Have Lived a Worthwhile Life

And what I am doing about it this week/month:

Focus area:	**Action When:**	(Pages 38, 39)
....	....	
....	....	
....	....	
....	....	
....	....	
....	....	
....	....	
....	....	

Measurement

If you have experienced any churning while working on this chapter, remember to use the tools of Chapter 1 to centre and ground and reconnect deeply with what is most important to you.

Remember that transitions do not happen in a nice, neat, linear order. Often they involve taking two steps forward then one step back.

Each successful Consolidation inevitably leads to a new Separation as we pursue a new vision in pursuit of our purpose and values. The tools of *Inner Leadership* enable us to do this in a way that deepens our understanding and our abilities all the while.

Having read Chapter 7 and completed the exercises, how well-prepared are you now to maintain your own inspiration and that of your team as you journey towards the outcome you chose in Chapter 4? (0-10)	

What differences will this make in your life? Professionally? Personally?	
What benefits will that bring? Emotionally? Financially?	
How valuable is that to you?	

PROGRESS REVIEW

Inner Leadership provides a step by step process for dealing with uncertainty. Each step builds on what came before, making you and your organisation more resilient and antifragile.

Use the charts on the following two pages to enter your current performance (0-10) for each of the seven competencies of inner leadership. Copy the scores you gave yourself at the beginning of each chapter into the next table. Then calculate the improvement you have made in each area.

Remember that metrics are never an end in themselves: they are only an indicator, a proxy, for something more important. Good leadership is fundamentally unmeasurable and only you can know how well you are leading yourself to where you want to be. Treat these numbers as a tool for reflection and a guide to help you lead yourself to where you want to be.

Current performance, having completed the workbook (pages 14, 20, 28, 44, 54, 68, 92):

Inner Leadership Skill or State:

Ready						
Inspired						
Determined						
Directed						
Optimistic						
Sure						
Deeply Centred and Grounded						
Churning						
Chapter: 1	2	3	4	5	6	7

How you rated yourself at the start of each chapter (pages 1, 15, 21, 29, 45, 55, 69):

Inner Leadership Skill or State:

Ready						
Inspired						
Determined						
Directed						
Optimistic						
Sure						
Deeply Centred and Grounded						
Churning						
Chapter: 1	2	3	4	5	6	7

Use this chart to show the improvements you have made in each chapter, by subtracting your original score from your current score:

Inner Leadership Skill or State:

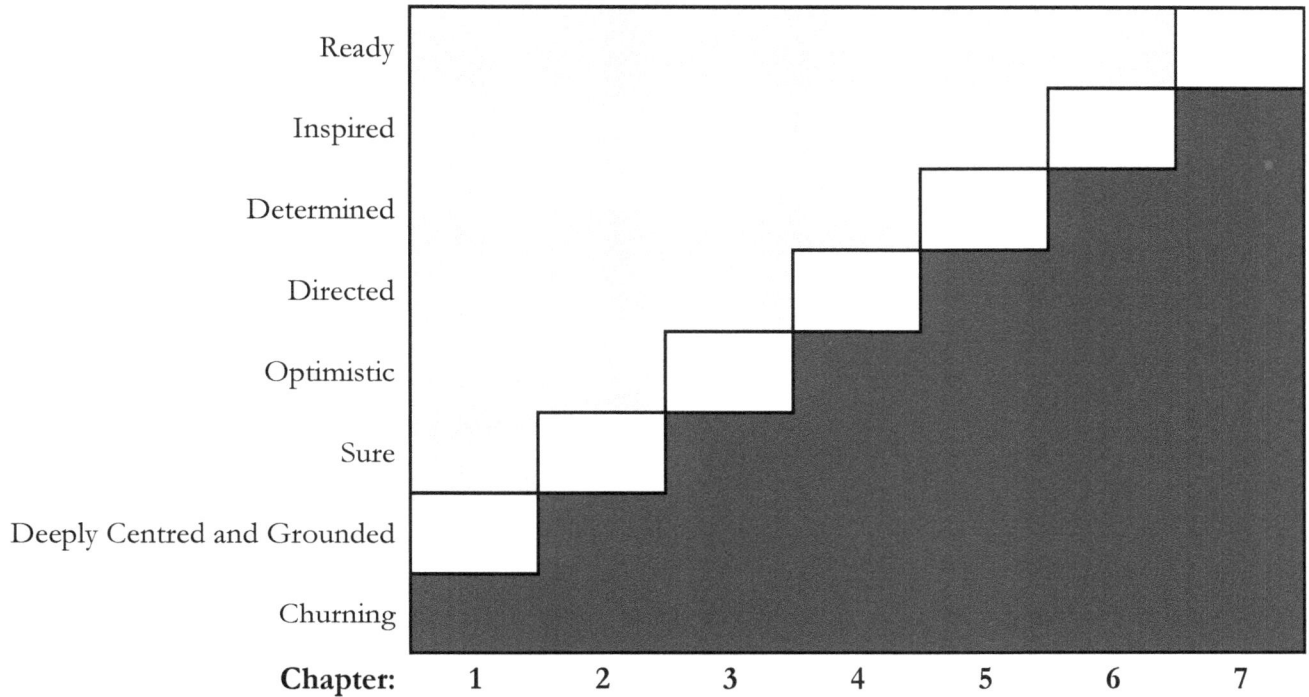

| | Ready | Inspired | Determined | Directed | Optimistic | Sure | Deeply Centred and Grounded | Churning |

Chapter: 1   2   3   4   5   6   7

Where have you made the greatest improvements? Was this what you expected (see page viii)? Where do you still want to improve?

Remember, a true leader creates more leaders, so if it will help you to achieve your purpose, values, current vision, or to live a worthwhile life please share this book.

THE NEXT LEVEL

As we practice the tools of *Inner Leadership* over time so we become more skilful at each of them. Greater skill at one competency also enhances the next and so we move faster round the cycle of *Inner Leadership*, improving our abilities with each completed circuit.

This chapter shifts our attention away from applying the individual tools on to managing the process as a whole.

This enables us to create three further benefits: joy for ourselves, antifragile competitive advantage for our organisations, and a more stable and generative business ecosystem and economy (created by 'igniting the organisation').

Seven Capabilities of Inner Leadership

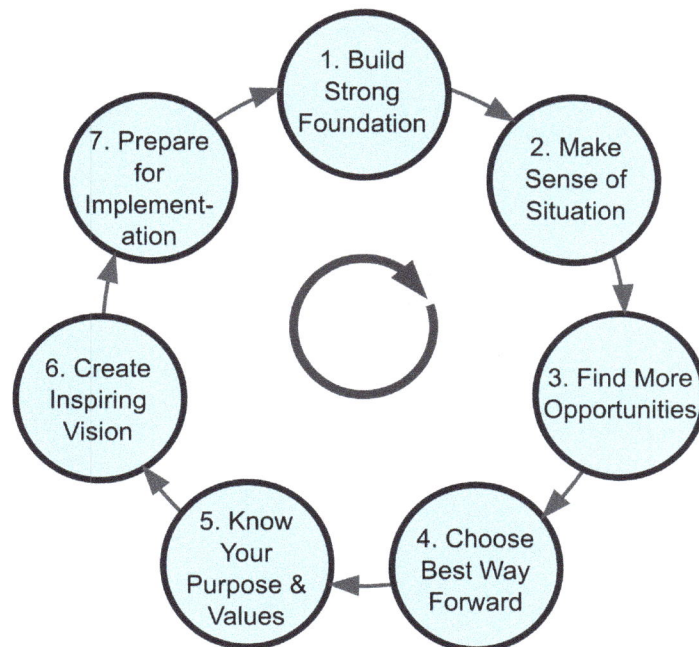

Joy

Pages 135-138 of *Inner Leadership* describe how joy comes when we focus on what matters most to us and let go of what does not. Joy comes when we choose our attitude and response to our situation and start to make a meaningful life out of an ordinary one.

The details vary from person to person but broadly there are three stages:
1. Knowing what is important to us
2. Finding ways to put that into practice, given the realities we face
3. Implementing those plans

Joy comes when we have strong capabilities in all three areas and cycle through them repeatedly.

Are you happy with your current abilities in these areas or do you want to improve any of them? Treat these questions as prompts and guides to find the actions that will bring the improvements you seek.

Knowing What is Important to Us:

Know our purpose and values (5) (Chapter numbers in brackets.)	How well do you know your purpose and values? To what extent do you apply them each day, especially when taking decisions? Would it be useful to review your purpose and values or update them?
Deepen our connection with ourselves (1)	How much time do you spend deepening your connection with yourself (pages 8-13 of *Inner Leadership*)? How effective is that? Would it be useful to spend more time on this or try a different approach?
Know what it will take for us to live a worthwhile life (4)	Do you know what it will take for you to have lived a worthwhile life? How much do you apply this knowledge in the choices you make?

Converting Our Priorities into Action Plans:

Finding more opportunities (3)	How well do you remember to look for all ten types of opportunity in a situation? How well do you find them? Would it be useful to improve this skill?
Making ourselves open to the possibilities (3)	Do you have a serendipity mindset? Do you review what went well at the end of each day? Do you thank and praise others? Do you use the Morning Pages? Do you explicitly look for people who might see your 'problem' as an opportunity?
Building a worthwhile life (4)	Do you use the building blocks of what a worthwhile life looks like to you to set priorities? Are you clear what '10' looks like in each case? Does that inspire you? Do you do something towards each one every month, week, or day? Do you spend appropriate amounts of time on each area? Is there a gap? Do you ask your 86-year-old self for advice?
Choosing appropriate next steps (4)	Do you use your knowledge of your purpose, values, and worthwhile life to guide you forward?

Implementing Our Plans:

Having trouble getting started (4)	Do you ever find yourself blocked by fear, overthinking, or not knowing who you want to become? Would it be useful to spend time overcoming or skirting around those barriers? Would it be useful to choose an objective that is easier to achieve so that you can complete a cycle of *Inner Leadership*, then learn and repeat?
Having trouble maintaining momentum (7, 6, 5)	Are you managing your transitions? Does your vision-story inspire you? If not, why not? What is missing? Are you using your values to guide your decisions in an uncertain world? Does your purpose call to you? How does what you are working on contribute to your purpose?
Getting distracted on to issues that are not priorities for you (1, 2, 5)	Do you get distracted by issues that are not important to you? Do you "Stop to throw stones at every dog that barks"? When issues arise, do you take time to centre and ground? Do you have a strong anchor to return to? Have you let go of your shoulds and other mis-blinks? Before you allocate time and energy to an issue, do you check whether it matters to your purpose, values, and worthwhile life?

Choosing too much of a stretch target / finding more support (4, 8)	Are you being too optimistic or idealistic? Is your chosen way forward too much of a stretch for the way reality is now? Would it be useful to choose a goal that fits better with the way external reality is now? Or to focus on strengthening your inner leadership to match your aims? What is the equivalent of your 'cello' today and where are there people who are longing to hear you play it?

Accelerating the Cycle of *Inner Leadership*:

Our ultimate aim is to be able to move quickly and seamlessly around each cycle of *Inner Leadership*	How can you best move faster round the cycle of *Inner Leadership*? Are there any competencies that stand out as relative weak spots for you, preventing you from completing each cycle of learning? If so, how will you develop them, when? Or is your priority now to let go of trying to improve in any one area and focus instead on moving faster through multiple cycles of *Inner Leadership*, learning by doing as you go?

Antifragile Competitive Advantage

Most organisations implement strategic change by following a linear process: they identify an issue, create a plan to deal with it, and then implement that plan.

The first level of antifragility comes when we make the change process circular. Managing transitions closes the loop by boosting the identification of future issues. It also improves implementation.

Full antifragility then arises when we use purpose and values to align and accelerate the four stages of change and use those four stages, in turn, to review the purpose and values and either embed them more deeply in the organisation or update them.

Pages 140-142 of *Inner Leadership* describe how antifragile competitive advantage arises when we combine the following five key competencies or capabilities:

1. Leaders and people who are able to identify (in a timely way) issues that require action and those that do not
2. Teams able to create robust plans to address those issues
3. Teams and a receptive organisation able to implement change programmes quickly, efficiently, and effectively
4. Leaders and people who are able to manage their transitions
5. A culture that uses each completed cycle of change to reinforce or develop its core purpose, values, attitudes, and behaviours

Cycle of Leadership for Antifragile Competitive Advantage

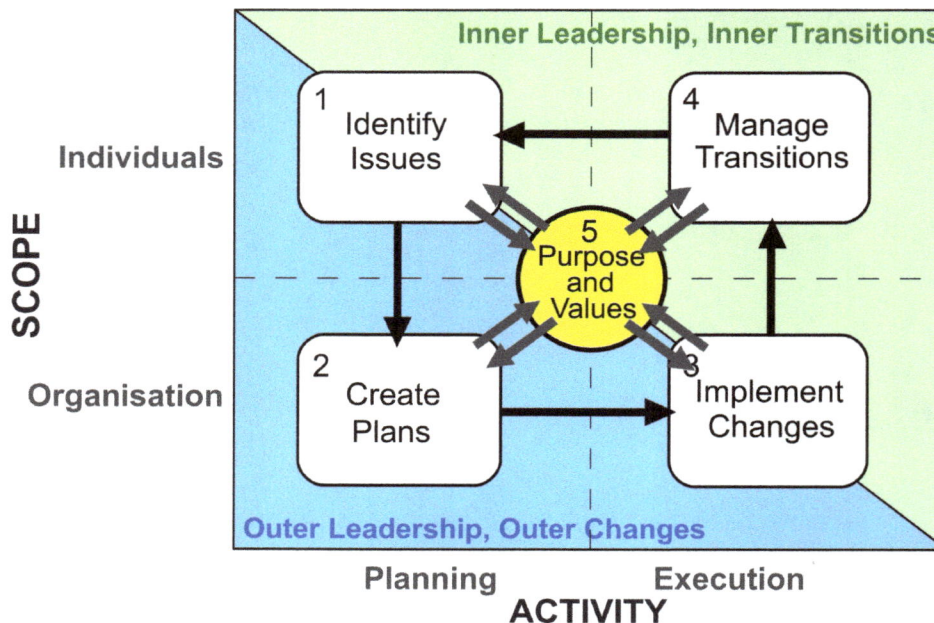

Use the following questions to assess your current performance at these five competencies and identify priorities for action to develop antifragile competitive advantage in yourself and/or your organisation.

Choose appropriately-sized next steps, starting from wherever you are today.

Competency 1: Identify Issues

Do you, your leaders, and people currently raise issues in an appropriate and timely way? (0-10)	
Is there room for improvement? If so where?	Consider issues raised late, time wasted on unimportant issues, length of time taken to decide whether or not to address an issue.
What trends will drive performance* over the next two years? (*Your performance or organisation performance)	
In two years' time, will there be more issues to consider, fewer, or the same? Is this the same for all parts of the organisation?	
Will it become important for you, your leaders, or people to be able to raise and prioritise more issues more quickly? Which groups of people most need to improve?	
How can you develop these people's abilities?	Consider introducing explicit triage processes, using purpose, values, attitudes, and behaviours to provide focus and alignment.
What actions will you take, when? (What's your vision-story for the changes?)	

Competency 2: Create Plans

How well do you, your leaders, and people currently create plans to address the issues you face? (0-10)	
Is there room for improvement? If so where?	Consider the time/resources taken to create a plan and how robust the plans turn out to be.
What trends will drive performance* over the next two years? (*Your performance or organisation performance)	
In two years' time, will the external (and internal) environment will be more predictable, less, or about the same? Is this the same for all parts of the organisation?	
Will it become easier or more difficult to create change plans or about the same? Which groups of people most need to improve?	
How can you develop these people's abilities?	Consider using purpose, values, attitudes, and behaviours to provide focus and alignment.
What actions will you take, when? (What's your vision-story for the changes?)	

Competency 3: Implement Change

How successfully do you, your leaders, and people currently implement change programmes? (0-10)	
Is there room for improvement? If so where?	As well as whether projects are on time and on budget, consider flexibility/robustness to changes and time taken for new business models/operating procedures to reach intended performance.
What trends will drive performance* over the next two years? (*Your performance or organisation performance)	
In two years' time, will the rate of external change be greater, smaller, or about the same? Is this the same for all parts of the organisation?	Will there be more need for change or less? Will individual changes be bigger or smaller?
Will this make it easier or more difficult to implement change, or about the same? Which groups of people most need to change?	Consider efficiency, effectiveness, adaptability, speed, and the time taken for new operating models to reach intended performance. What works better: few large changes or many small ones?
How can you develop these people's abilities?	Consider the extent to which you involve the organisation in designing and implementing the change. Consider using purpose, values, attitudes, and behaviours to provide focus and alignment.
What actions will you take, when? (What's your vision-story for the changes?)	

Competency 4: Manage Transitions

How good are you, your leaders, and people currently at managing the transitions associated with change? (0-10)	Are there problems with morale, retention, or implementing change?
Is there room for improvement? If so where?	Consider Separation, crossing the Threshold, Consolidation.
What trends will drive performance* over the next two years? (*Your performance or organisation performance)	
In two years' time, will the emotional and psychological demands on people be larger, smaller, or about the same? Is this the same for all parts of the organisation?	
Will this make the ability to manage transitions more useful, less useful, or about the same? Which groups of people most need to change?	Consider morale, employee retention, speed/ease of implementation of change, time taken for changes to reach full productivity.
How can you develop these people's abilities?	Consider using purpose, values, attitudes, and behaviours to provide focus and alignment. Consider training others in the skills of *Inner Leadership*.
What actions will you take, when? (What's your vision-story for the changes?)	

Competency 5: Reinforce and Develop Purpose and Values

How deeply are purpose and values currently embedded in the daily decisions and actions of yourself, your leaders, and people? (0-10)	
Is there room for improvement? If so where?	Consider the extent to which groups are able to act independently, quickly, yet remain aligned. Consider not only whether purpose and values are defined but also whether they are used in decision-making.
What trends will drive performance* over the next two years? (*Your performance or organisation performance)	
In two years' time, will levels of volatility, uncertainty, and complexity be smaller, larger, or about the same? Is this the same for all parts of the organisation?	
Will this make purpose and values more useful, less useful, or about the same? Which groups of people most need to change?	Purpose and values attract people to join, provide motivation to address issues, plus higher productivity, alignment, and enjoyment.
How can you develop these people's abilities?	Consider Chapters 4-7 of *Inner Leadership*. Consider explicitly including purpose and values in decision making, with periodic reviews of how purpose and values have been put into action to reinforce or update what they mean in practice.
What actions will you take, when? (What's your vision-story for the changes?)	

A Stable Generative Economy

The tools of *Inner Leadership* are designed to bring about change in individuals but they can also create change at the level of the economy. When several companies align around a shared purpose they form a purpose-led business ecosystem. This generates three business benefits that multiply across the ecosystem and then out into the economy.

The first benefit is higher productivity.

The second is greater agility and antifragile competitive advantage.

The third benefit comes when people who have 'let go' come to work in organisations that are run to be antifragile (see pages 145-146 of *Inner Leadership*). This is 'igniting the organisation'. When one or more businesses in an ecosystem do this the effects ripple across the productivity, competitiveness, and adaptability of the whole ecosystem – and ultimately out into the economy.

To achieve an improvement in these areas, start by asking yourself these questions.

What type of improvement are you most seeking: productivity, agility/antifragile competitive advantage, or to generatively 'ignite' an organisation and the whole ecosystem? Why?	
Are you seeking to create change in your own organisation or in other member(s) of the ecosystem? Why?	
Is your organisation the central unit of the ecosystem (for example, like Unilever) or are you a supplier to that organisation? This affects how you might go about creating the change you seek.	

Productivity

Gallup showed that companies with highly engaged workforces "outperform their peers by 147% in earnings per share." When a business aligns with a purpose-led ecosystem it brings inspiration and meaning, raising quality and lowering costs (and so benefitting the entire ecosystem).

If your main priority is to increase productivity, use the earlier section on joy to think through how you might best introduce and activate meaning for the target organisation. Which group of people do you most need to inspire? Which tools would bring the most immediate benefits? What are your next steps to make this happen?

Which group of people would bring the organisation most benefit from learning inner leadership? Which group would be most open to learning inner leadership?	Consider: key leaders, a 'diagonal slice' of key employees, or all employees in a business unit

Which inner leadership tools would bring the most immediate value? (Chapters in brackets.)

Knowing What is Important (1, 4, 5) Consider current performance, needed performance, action plan, upsides/downsides.	
Converting Those Priorities into Action Plans: (3, 4) Consider current performance, needed performance, action plan, upsides/downsides.	
Implementing Plans: (4, 5, 6, 7, 1, 2) Consider current performance, needed performance, action plan, upsides/downsides.	

Antifragile Competitive Advantage

A company that aligns with purpose becomes more agile. When several firms align around the same purpose it strengthens their competitive advantage with scale and robustness, while retaining agility.

If your main priority is to build antifragile competitive advantage, first identify your target organisation. Then use the section on Antifragile Competitive Advantage (page 102) to think through which competency(/ies) you want to improve and how to go about introducing that change. What are your next steps?

Current performance, needed performance	Consider: Changes you seek, Target group(s) of people, Ways to achieve the changes, Upsides/downsides, Vision-stories, Preferred approach, Your next steps
1) Identify Issues	
2) Create Plans	
3) Implementation	
4) Manage Transitions	
5) Reinforce and Develop Purpose and Values	

Igniting the Organisation

When people who are skilled at inner leadership work in roles that match their personal purpose, something magical happens. Now these people are no longer 'doing a job' – they are building themselves, fulfilling their purpose, self-actualising. They bring more energy and talent to their roles. And as they grow their talents, so they become more likely to generate the innovations that drive success. If the organisation is run to be antifragile, these effects are amplified. Repeated across an ecosystem, each 'joyful' person becomes a source of innovation and responsiveness – a generative node within an antifragile network – that makes the entire ecosystem more stable, responsive, adaptive, and generative. Self-actualisation happens when a person knows who they are and the unique skills they bring, and also finds a place that enables them to put those skills to maximum effect. An ecosystem that provides this is 'ignited'.

To 'ignite' your target organisation, ask yourself whether the priority now is: to generate more self-directed **people** (see the above sections on Productivity and Joy); to make the **organisation** more anti-fragile (see above); or to increase the **alignment** between people and organisation (by changing roles).

Start by deciding your scope: does the appropriate next step focus on a few key leaders, the critical 2%-5% of all employees, or perhaps an entire purpose-driven business unit or group?

What **scope** is appropriate for you to focus on now? Why? A few key leaders? The critical 2%-5% of employees? All employees in a unit? Other?	
To what extent have these **people** currently developed their inner leadership? (0-10) To what extent are they aware of and practicing what it will take for them to have lived a worthwhile life, their personal purpose, their values, their key qualities and the ways they love applying them?	
To what extent does the **organisation** support them in putting this into practice? (0-10) To what extent does the organisation provide a consistent antifragile environment, aligned around purpose and values?	

How strong is the **alignment** between people and positions? Does the role enable them to apply their best qualities in the ways they love to create their ideal world and to live a worthwhile life?	
Is the priority to: - Develop the inner leadership skills of the target group (so they know their purpose and values more clearly and how to put them into practice), or - Change the organisation culture, or - Create better match and alignment between people and positions?	Connect more of these people with their personal purpose and how to put that into practice Change the way the organisation is managed, to give this group of people more freedom and support to follow their passions Match these already highly self-directed people with roles where they will have transformative impacts on organisation performance
What is your vision-story for following this approach?	
What actions will you take, when?	

www.ingramcontent.com/pod-product-compliance
Lightning Source LLC
Chambersburg PA
CBHW050243220326
41598CB00048B/7492